God bless!

Sept. '09

An EVENT to REMEMBER

DESIGNING SPECTACULAR SPECIAL OCCASIONS

JERRY SIBAL

Founder of DESIGN FUSION

with

ROGER YEE

Photographs by

MOON LEE

Foreword by

MARILYN HORNE

STEWART, TABORI & CHANG | NEW YORK

Published in 2009 by
Stewart, Tabori & Chang
An imprint of Harry N. Abrams, Inc.

Library of Congress Cataloging-in-
Publication Data:
Sibal, Jerry.
  An event to remember : designing
spectacular special occasions / by Jerry Sibal.
     p. cm.
  Includes bibliographical references and
index.
  ISBN 978-1-58479-790-6 (alk. paper)
1. Special events--Planning. 2. Weddings--
Planning. 3. Corporate meetings--Planning. 4.
Wedding decorations. 5. Floral decorations.
6.Party decorations. I.Title.
  GT3405.S545 2009
  394.2—dc22   2009002292

Editor: Kristen Latta
Designer: Susi Oberhelman
Production Manager: Tina Cameron

The text of this book was composed in
Folio and Electra.

Printed and bound in China
10 9 8 7 6 5 4 3 2 1

ABRAMS
THE ART OF BOOKS SINCE 1949
115 West 18th Street
New York, NY 10011
www.hnabooks.com

CONTENTS

I DEDICATE THIS BOOK TO:

My loving departed parents, Jose Ong and Valentina Sibal, for
nurturing me and encouraging me to become an artist

My beloved lifetime partner, Edwin Josue, for inspiration,
unconditional love, and for being the guiding light

My brother and sisters, Josie, Johnny, Susan, and Elizabeth, and
their families, for encouragement and joy

FOREWORD

I love flowers—I never want to be without them! They cheer me up and brighten my day. The love of nature is one of the most important things in my life. When Jerry designed the table decorations for my 75th birthday dinner at New York's Plaza Grand Ballroom in January 2009, all had been kept secret from me before the event, so that I would be supremely surprised. I walked into the ballroom and literally *gasped*! Jerry is a unique artist and brought much more than floral design to the event. It was an extraordinary feast for the eyes.

In the pages that follow, your eyes too will be able to feast on many of the glorious events that Jerry has designed. It seems that there is no event—grand or intimate—that Jerry can't elevate to the level of artistry. When it is someone's wedding or bat mitzvah or 75th birthday, no detail is too small. In this book, you will see just how Jerry fills any space with the most unique special touches, the most spectacular flowers, and the most creative designs. Jerry's clients' interests run the gamut and so does his work. From an outdoor wedding in California to a celebration at New York's revered Rainbow Room to a holiday dinner in his own apartment, Jerry brings unparalleled skill and vision to any event.

I hope you will be as thrilled as I have been to see what Jerry can do, and perhaps you will take from him inspiration for your own special occasion. I know I will be inspired by my unforgettable birthday celebration for years to come.

What you see in Jerry's drawing is what you get in reality.

—PAULETTE WOLF, Paulette Wolf Events and Entertainment, Inc.

INTRODUCTION

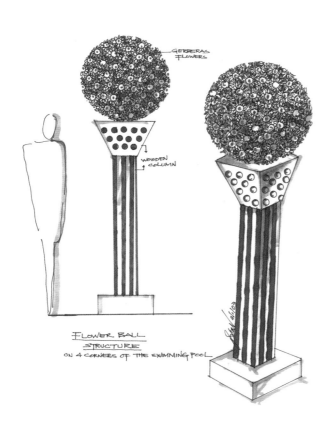

GERBERAS
FLOWERS

WOODEN
COLUMN

FLOWER BALL
STRUCTURE
ON 4 CORNERS OF THE SWIMMING POOL

New York is an exciting place to live. Companies, families, and individuals in and around this great city entrust the design of their special events—corporate events, cultural events, weddings, and other social events—to me so that I can create unique environments and floral designs to make these occasions impressive and memorable. There's never a dull moment in my business. Every day I meet people eager to explore something different and experience something new.

I've been asked so often how I combine art, architecture, floral design, and performing arts to produce magical settings that I decided to write a book about it. This book can serve as a source of information and inspiration to guide you in planning your own special event. In the pages that follow, you will see what can be done with ordinary spaces as well as landmarks to give them astonishing new personalities, and you will read how I work with my clients step by step to turn their dreams into realities.

My inspiration comes from a lifetime of people, things, and places that make a strong impression on me. I recall them sometimes by means of photographs or other print or electronic images. Quite often, however, I just recall them at will because they reveal a strong association with an assignment I am taking on. It's fair to say that designers and artists regularly see the world as it *could* be, whereas most people see the world for what it *is*, so they are accustomed to recalling a lot of images almost by habit.

As for my philosophy, I regard design as a collaborative effort. As a creative individual, I know I provide the primary sources of inspiration for my work. Yet creating an environment for an organization, individual, or family is not exactly like creating art. I cannot design anything for my clients without fully accounting for their goals and resources, along with the physical spaces where they want to hold their events. No design I prepare is successful unless it performs as my clients have requested, using the facilities they have provided for my use.

I also want to acknowledge the importance of nature in my work. To me, nature is the bridge between the spiritual world of humanity and the physical world that nurtures us. You don't need to share my view of nature as a divine creation. But who can fail to appreciate the unique beauty, power, economy, and originality of nature's forms? When I choose floral and other natural and organic materials to combine with man-made materials, I never cease to wonder at the superiority of nature in giving my work its unique qualities.

WEDDINGS

WHEN YOU ARE AS FORTUNATE AS I AM TO WORK WITH couples and families to design the perfect setting for a wedding, you truly appreciate why this is one of the happiest occasions in life. It's not just about a bride and groom beginning a new life together. It's about families giving away their babies, and families forming new relationships that can last a lifetime. • Under such circumstances, I feel compelled to do everything possible to help create the perfect day. In making plans with the mothers of the brides, I strive to be sensitive to their feelings, attentive to what they need, and accommodating to their often quite detailed requests. I'm not exaggerating when I say some mothers start planning their daughters' weddings from birth. • Every wedding is as distinctive and unique as the couples and families involved. So I begin the design of a wedding by getting to know my clients' personalities and social backgrounds, their special interests and other concerns, and the program of festivities they wish to hold. Of course, that's just the start of a carefully orchestrated effort. Before the big day actually arrives, I will shape my design according to such key factors as the season of the year and the hours of the day, the venues where ceremonies and celebrations will occur, the choice of attire, food and beverage, music and other entertainment, and the timing when specific activities must commence. • I won't deny that staging the perfect wedding requires a substantial effort. But the joy and satisfaction it brings to my clients and to me go beyond description. I become a family friend in the process, going all out to give them beauty that totally surrounds them, sights, sounds, and scents to savor, and memories to cherish forever.

LOVE IN BLOOM

Made for each other: it's a lovely sentiment that's frequently conferred on brides and grooms. It's also a goal I strive to achieve in each one-of-a-kind environment I design for a wedding party. Abigail and Heath's wedding at the Capitale in New York's historic and now trendy Lower East Side demonstrates how satisfying a good match between a space and an event can be. The Capitale is a grand Beaux Arts building, the expression of confident, successful people who knew who they were and what they wanted of life. My clients and I decided that maximizing the beauty and drama from its Roman-scaled interior for the wedding festivities seemed to call for equally bold gestures.

To begin, I greeted guests with an escort-card table dominated by phalaenopsis orchids and pink roses in a sculptured arrangement. The circular chuppah, whose shape fit perfectly with the Renaissance geometry of the architecture, was defined by flowers and sheer fabric, a crystal candelabra suspended in the center, and concealed light sources that made the center of the ceremony the main source of illumination for the entire room. The challenge of this event was transforming the room in only an hour to reflect an autumn mood. At the guest tables, I designed lofty, big branch arrangements from which I suspended crystals, softening their impact with clusters of fall flower bouquets at the base. Pillar candles of varying heights and glass candle holders created a dramatic glow on the table setting. I think it's safe to say bride and groom conquered the Capitale, which happily surrendered to them.

ROMANCE IN HALF MOON BAY

Dating back to 1840, Half Moon Bay is the oldest town in San Mateo County, California, and you can see traces of its past in the historic buildings that coexist with native foliage, abundant wildlife, and a rugged coast overlooking the Pacific Ocean. I found it to be a place of unexpected charms, including a historic Main Street, two wineries, major flower growers, horseback riding, and surfing.

In planning a perfect outdoor wedding, it is imperative to keep your guests comfortable so that they simply enjoy the beautiful scenery. It is also important to have a backup plan in case of rain, and consider the wind and sound factor.

Though the climate tends to be cool, I helped Andrew and Michelle design a simple garden wedding for 100 guests that would be as crisp, fresh, and colorful as Half Moon Bay itself.

The existing white arbor on the garden was filled with purple hydrangeas, pink flowering plants, and tons of phalaenopsis orchids. The floor was scattered with loose rose petals to create the perfect setting for a garden wedding. I created simple table settings focusing on centerpieces that comprised hydrangea, dahlias, phalaenopsis orchids, peonies, eucalyptus, and sweet peas planted in baskets and other rustic containers. Mother Nature herself collaborated with me by giving the wedding party an atypically warm, sunny, and altogether glorious day for the event.

A THOUSAND POINTS OF LIGHT

It is fortunate that many old banking halls have been reborn as event venues, including New York's Gotham Hall. We could never duplicate these magnificent spaces today. For a recent wedding in Gotham Hall, the couple and their families wanted to hold a classic event, and I was pleased to create a timeless design for them that drew on a palette of purple, lavender, pink, and white to enrich the already spectacular space. In the entry foyer, guests found their place cards in a setting highlighted by a modern composition of flowers in glass vases set at three different heights. For the great hall, I combined a silver julep cup as the flower vessel with gold candelabra to make a stately tabletop, filling the cup with dense, low clusters of peonies, roses, and orchids to encourage people to enjoy each other's company. Since the wedding celebration was taking place in Gotham Hall, I selected tall tapered candles, which guests could easily see around, to acknowledge the vaulted ceiling high above the couple and their party.

A ROYAL WEDDING

More than a few brides have dreamed of holding their weddings in palaces. While New York doesn't have any such heirlooms from King George III that I'm aware of, the fabled Metropolitan Club on tony Fifth Avenue can certainly play the part convincingly. Designing for the bride and groom in this landmark gave me both the chance to realize a dream for the couple and to rediscover the brilliance of America's architects and builders a century ago. How does one compete with such splendor? I took a contrarian's point of view and transformed the architecture into a supportive backdrop—a magnificent one, to be sure— illuminated largely by the reflected light from the wedding's activities.

To dramatize each stage of the event, I focused lighting on the chuppah, where the nuptial ceremony was performed, designed custom-made lampshades to visually lower the high ceiling for cocktails, and spotlighted the centerpieces on tables in the main dining room. Of course, the floral arrangements were critical for capturing and diffusing light. For the chuppah, I used white orchids on sheer gold fabric, a crown filled with roses and hydrangeas, and tall pillar candles, a display reprised in the aisle with tall candelabras bearing candles and flowers. For the dining tables, I paired low floral arrangements of rich flowers and pomegranate fruits resting on a cut crystal bow, created to enhance intimate conversations among the guests, with high floral arrangements elevated to establish the wedding party's presence in the room. I think every couple should feel like royalty at their wedding.

AN ART-DECO WEDDING

For a wedding at Miami Beach's luxurious Hotel Setai, I adapted the hotel's Art Deco style (it began as the famed Dempsey Vanderbilt Hotel in the late 1930s) as the design theme for nuptials with a twist. I created a black-and-white Art Moderne environment to explore the distinctive vision of Hollywood in the 1940s.

The wedding ceremony began at the Temple Emmanuel with a timeless, Neoclassical gesture, featuring a chuppah with Doric columns, arching canopy, and garlands with jewel-toned flowers such as purple hydrangeas, burgundy peonies, cymbidium orchids, and red roses.

For the dining and dancing at the Hotel Setai, I called for square, rectangular, and circular tables to create an unconventional floor plan, raised platforms for lounges and stage performances to give elevation and focus to the tented space, mounted a crystal chandelier above a custom-designed vinyl dance floor to impart an exclusive touch, and installed mirrors draped with

sprays of white hydrangeas as backdrops to increase the sense of depth. There were two tabletop designs: one focused on a black round bowl and another centered on a custom-made square crystal lampshade, each filled with clusters of white anemones and hydrangeas and pillar candles that sat on top of a mirror table.

A Chicago-based party planner and I worked with the bride and her family to plan the wedding down to the smallest detail. Guests were greeted with fireworks as they walked between twin rows of illuminated columns to the tented space. Two white storks perched on little hilltops of white hydrangeas stood guard beside the tiered all-white cupcake wedding cake.

After the dinner dance at the tent outside the hotel, my team struck down the entire tent décor used in the festivities. The formality of the Art Moderne–style décor at the wedding was contrasted with a casual, outdoor environment in the same space for the next morning's brunch, sort of like guiding a magic carpet ride down to a soft landing. The design scheme was simple and straightforward, combining outdoor furniture upholstered in colorful Pucci fabrics with coffee tables and sit-down tables accented by rich, jewel-toned floral pieces. When guests took their seats, they found themselves in a relaxing, beach-like setting, in full view of a blue sky and Miami's white sand beach.

ON TOP OF THE WORLD

New Yorkers aren't really that different from tourists in feeling spellbound and enchanted when they visit the Rainbow Room, enthroned atop the GE Building, the pinnacle of New York's Rockefeller Center.

From this showcase of Art Deco art, architecture, and design, the sophisticated world celebrated by George Gershwin and Cole Porter seems at your feet. That's why I approached the design for Michael and Eunyoung's wedding in the Rainbow Room with subtlety and understatement.

Since the space embodied the very same urbane and stylish mood sought by the couple and their families for the event, I crafted centerpieces high and low to reflect the rich ornamentation and breath-taking verticality of the Art Deco New York world that surrounded us. The tall arrangements gave the wedding its signature look, featuring white pheleanopsis orchids, lilies, white hydrangeas, and roses on crystal candelabras. It all added up to a glamorous night on the town for the wedding couple and their party, celebrating in their perch on top of the world.

REVERENCE AND REVELRY

The decoration of a sanctuary for a wedding calls for reverence and humility, since many houses of worship are already magnificent spaces enriched with frescoes, mosaics, statuary, and architectural ornamentation. Yet even the simplest floral design can have a meaningful impact on the most baroque interior.

For the wedding of Karen and David at New York's Church of Our Savior, I felt that two big arrangements featuring cherry blossoms would introduce a distinct mood that would reach its zenith at the altar with two medium-sized floral arrangements of lilies and roses. Wonderful as the church was in its everyday splendor, I'm pleased that the arrangements added subtle grace notes. The tall cherry blossoms created such an expansive feeling that I brought them into the reception dining room as well, where their profile kept everyone's spirits high.

MODERN IN MANHATTAN

Columbus Circle, which anchors the southwest corner of New York's Central Park, has never been the same since the AOL Time Warner Center opened. Suddenly, a modern urban complex offering a soaring atrium, luxury hotel and condominiums, high-end retailing, fine dining, corporate offices, and performing arts venues has revived a once-forgotten neighborhood bordering Frederick Law Olmsted's masterpiece.

Collaborating with Melanie Arden of Melarosa to design a contemporary wedding in the grand ballroom of the Mandarin Oriental hotel, we were as eager as our client to create an environment that would complement the spare and elegantly refined architecture. Our concept incorporated straight lines of white roses and sheer white fabric to give a clean and modern look to the chuppah and a group of high and low square pillar candles on a metal stand decorated with flowers as aisle décor.

After the ceremony, the whole ballroom had been transformed to the contemporary feel of dining in a spring garden scene. Tall cherry blossoms, green hydrangeas, vibernium exploding from tall glass vases with wheatgrass below on the tables, and purple uplighting set the tone for the entire event.

SPRINGTIME IN A BOTANICAL GARDEN

Just contemplate a springtime wedding in the magnificent conservatory of New York's beloved Brooklyn Botanic Garden, an urban horticultural and living musuem. It sounds almost too perfect, doesn't it? I can vouch for at least one, because I was honored with a commission from an inspired family to design it. In celebrating the start of new life after a long winter, the promise of unlimited possibilities, and the simple, wholesome freshness of youth, I designed a deliberately understated setting based on highlighting each table with simple yet elegant clusters of peonies, roses, and green hydrangeas. These clusters lent their soft, pastel hues to an otherwise restrained color palette of white chairs, white table linen, and silver julep cups, which I included to hold the flowers during the festivities and accompany guests home as mementos. For a touch of sparkle, I placed white pillar candles among the clusters, where their flames could symbolize the hopes and ideals of the nascent season for the happy couple and their guests.

THE TROPICS MEET TRADITION

Can tropical flora achieve harmony with neoclassical architecture? I think the two go together marvelously.

I was asked to create a vibrant atmosphere for Jason and Lauren's wedding that would feature tropical flowers inside the sumptuous interior of Manhattan's Capitale, a former banking hall. For the escort-card table, I constructed tall tree branches decorated with hanging white orchid leis, glittering crystals, and a sea of green spider mums. The two-ring suspended chuppah symbolized the union of a couple and were decorated with white orchids, green foliages, hanging crystals in the center, and draped sheer fabrics on the sides. After the ceremony, guests were led to the cocktail area while we transformed the main ballroom into a tropical paradise.

For the main dinner reception, I made three different styles of sculptural floral arrangements, one in white, one in red and gold, and one in fuchsia. Their impact was unmistakable, transforming the monumental rotunda into a lush environment recalling the conservatories that legendary families of the Gilded Age planted in their mansions. Playing the rich, jewel tones of exotic flowers against such timeless hues as copper, hunter green, and purple in the table settings and Indian silk brocade tablecloths, I completed the illusion of radiant tropical islands afloat in the darkened sea of the Capitale's floor.

EUROPEAN STYLE IN A LEGENDARY HOTEL

Certain places are so singular in character that to love them is to love both their basic architecture and their decorative style. It's certainly true for the ballroom in the penthouse of the venerable St. Regis Hotel, ensconced in midtown Manhattan close to Rockefeller Center, St. Patrick's Cathedral, and Central Park. Invited to design a setting for a wedding in the ballroom, I was moved by the Baroque style—so European and so confident in its vaulted ceiling, arched windows, and graceful ornamentation—that defines this airy space. I made the most of its charm by creating a centerpiece of blue and purple hydrangeas, salmon peonies, fuschia phalaenopsis orchids, and pink roses set in a glass modern bowl, placing it on a teal-colored damask tablecloth, and surrounding it with teal pillar candles mounted in crystal fluted candelabra. For the head table, I spread out masses of bouquet flowers of the same color scheme and flower materials with pillar and crystal votive candles to add elegance to the table setting.

SOCIAL EVENTS

I FEEL BLESSED THAT I AM ABLE TO HELP INDIVIDUALS, families, and friends to celebrate such key moments in their lives as birthdays, engagements, anniversaries, reunions, confirmations, the arrival of children, and the observance of holidays. Busy as we all are, we want and need to pause in our daily labors to mark important milestones among our families and friends. After all, what is life really about? • To give clients appropriate settings for their happy occasions, I spend time with them to learn who they and their guests are, what their special social events mean to them, and how they wish to celebrate these events. There are no formulas for appropriate designs, of course. Each social event is uniquely shaped by my clients, their celebration, and the venue they have chosen, and I tailor my design to suit them as ideally as I can. • No detail is too big or small when something like a 50th birthday or a baby christening is being commemorated. Will faded photographs from the college years be shown to spark fresh recollections? Is there a grandparent with a never-before-told story and a special gift to bestow? I'm always eager to add these precious jewels to the program and to accommodate them whenever possible in my design. Helping people to share key moments in their lives with others—especially in ways that become part of the family legacy or strengthen the bonds of friendship—keeps me eager and inspired to design my next social event.

A PERSONALIZED BAR MITZVAH

How would it feel to wake up on your birthday to discover that you are the center of the known universe, at least for one day? For Michael's bar mitzvah, his parents invited me to join them in producing just such an occasion for their son. We started with an exhibition space in New York City called the Metropolitan Pavilion that provided generic walls, ceilings, and floors—a clean slate for whatever we wished to do. Next came a schematic diagram of everything that would happen in the space. When the interior design, graphics, floral design, and special effects for the celebration were complete, Michael's family and friends would come to know and appreciate him as never before.

My design for the space focused on inventing different and imaginative ways to depict and display the letter M as a logo. As such, it unfolded like a movie

sequence. When guests entered the Metropolitan Pavilion, they saw two illuminated waterfalls with Michael's "M" logo on them. Then came an enormous black-and-white photograph of Michael bordered by a doorway framed in red curtains and a black-and-white checkerboard floor supporting three enormous, glowing white fiberglass vases topped by large balls of red roses. Once guests entered the doorway, they were greeted by an "M" logo constructed of roses and links of glass crystal, and lighted to throw a big, reflected "M" on the wall.

From here, guests entered the cocktail area, where white Lucite® bars and a white sofa lounge offered a quiet interlude and a moment's repose. But not for long. The pace quickened again in the main dining room, where guests passed illuminated tables, each displaying a one-of-a-kind floral structure, to find their tables on the periphery of a dance floor bearing an oversized image of the "M" logo in plaid. A final touch of whimsy was added to the children's table, which I decorated with a lively floral structure that included a spray of photos of Michael.

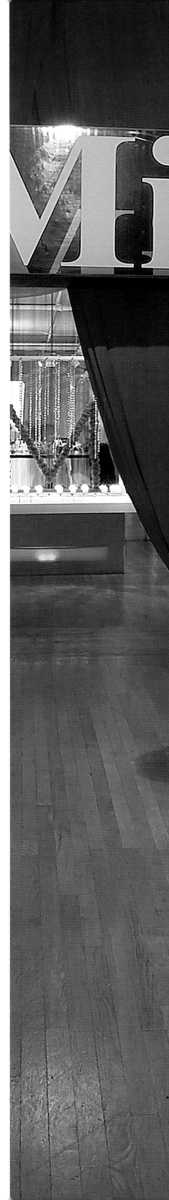

AN INTIMATE CHRISTMAS DINNER

Like so many of my clients, I enjoy hosting parties for family and friends at my home, which is in a modern apartment building on a major Manhattan thoroughfare. For a Christmas holiday dinner, I designed an environment to celebrate the joys of peace as well as the blessings of the earth, a composition I colored in shades of gold and green. It was sheer fun inventing ways to invest my apartment with holiday spirit. For the dining table, I ornamented evergreen boughs with glass birds, bird's feathers, bird's nests, and green plants such as lady's slipper, illuminating the results with pillar candles. I continued the theme by constructing a Christmas tree using natural and organic materials. Then I embellished the Murano glass chandelier with more holiday greens and glass birds. I didn't stop there, of course, but you can see how design and the fruits of man and nature invested my everyday space with magic.

Edwin Josue

Jerry Sibal

BRIDGE TO ADULTHOOD

It seems all little girls play dress up and experiment with make-up until suddenly they're not little girls any more. That's why I was so pleased to work with Clara and her family to design a special environment for her bat mitzvah celebration at the clubhouse of the Bryn Mawr Golf and Country Club in Chicago. They wanted a setting that was sophisticated and playful at the same time, remembering Clara's happy childhood and anticipating her exciting life as a young adult. In response, I designed a series of spaces to delight and inspire guests young and old.

Guests entering the lobby passed lively sprays of cherry blossoms atop pink-lighted Lucite® pedestals to gaze upon an oversized, wire mesh–formed ladies' bouquet in the center, rich in flowers, feathers, and hanging crystals, attended by sculptured, minimalist arrangements of white orchids in white vases. In the ballroom, I covered the chandeliers with square lampshades, set up a backdrop of textile designs by Pucci, and covered the dance floor with a contemporary graphic design framing Clara's name. For the children's room, I featured long tables, illuminated vases with cherry blossoms and carnations, and a play area defined by a semi-circular enclosure decorated in Pucci designs. Girls and boys of all ages had a wonderful time with Clara and her family.

A SOPHISTICATED SWEET SIXTEEN

Note cards, telephone calls, e-mail, or text messaging: What's your preference? Some of us are loyal to tradition while others are eager for the next big thing. There's no right or wrong here. Because social events are important expressions of personal beliefs and preferences, I encourage my clients to take pride in who they are and what they cherish in planning their special

occasions. Kiara and her family wanted an unconventional, contemporary, fashion-forward setting for her Sweet 16, and I was thrilled to design it for them.

As you can imagine, guests quickly realized what awaited them. At the entrance to the dining room, I placed a striking arrangement of tropical plants from which a dress form arose, enveloped in orchids and other flowers. On the guest tables, I planted tall tropical arrangements that conveyed the same bold sense of style from the entrance. Even if you had never met Kiara, you could enjoy the evocative tribute to this lively and talented young woman.

A PASSION FOR SPORTS

Young people are often the most passionate about things, and Max's bar mitzvah celebration at New York's venerable Pierre Hotel was emphatic about one young man's devotion to basketball. I must confess I had a ball serving Max and his family in designing the environment for this important coming-of-age celebration. For the design of the table centerpiece I actually inserted a real basketball inside a Lucite® casing with wheatgrass, resting on a structured, glowing light. I didn't stop there, of course. The dining room featured a big backdrop of a basketball player in motion on the wall. On the dance floor, guests saw yet another basketball. Max's family worked closely with me to accomplish this affectionate, funny, and honest tribute to a fine young man who is surely destined to accomplish a great deal on and off the court.

MOROCCO IN NEW YORK

If you could travel to anywhere on earth for a festive event, chances are you wouldn't stay home. Hoteliers and restaurateurs know this, and provide ample opportunities for us to escape to an exotic world that may be just around the corner. A faraway place can be surprisingly easy to conjure with good design. For Claire's New York bat mitzvah, her family liked the idea of a Moroccan-themed party.

To transform Studio 450's raw space, I suspended custom-made silk drapes and hanging lanterns from the ceiling and set out long tables with benches topped by richly upholstered cushions. Not leaving the least detail to chance, I combined more lanterns with clusters of flowers for floral arrangements at each table, and washed the space in a variety of lighting to produce just the right ambiance. Did Claire and her guests really believe they were partying in North Africa? Seeing is believing.

LIGHTING A NEW YORK LANDMARK

Do you believe that a memorable event must be ornate or complicated to succeed? I have good news for you. Sometimes the right thing to do is to go in the opposite direction. Take Nicole's bat mitzvah at the legendary Rainbow Room atop Rockefeller Center, New York's greatest Art Deco landmark. I designed the decor to give Nicole and her family their own personalized vision of the Rainbow Room to share with guests.

Envisioning a magical world based on lamps and lampshades, I combined lampshades that I designed and had custom fabricated with flowers that I draped in a cascade around the lamp columns and lamp bases. I encircled the lamp bases with pillar candles for a final flourish. Though the panoramic views of New York outside the windows inevitably claimed their share of attention, my clients happily found that the "lamps" also intrigued and delighted guests throughout the event, lending this event a distinctive quality other visitors to the Rainbow Room may never know for themselves.

CULTURAL EVENTS

YOU DON'T HAVE TO BE A HISTORIAN, PHILOSOPHER, OR economist to know that great nations prosper when their commercial enterprises and cultural institutions mutually support and learn from each other. I'm reminded of this every time I design a cultural event involving a performing arts company, a museum, a medical center, a school, a religious organization, or similar group. Events are an important way for cultural institutions to rally public support, reward outstanding service, connect with a larger constituency, or commemorate important moments or milestones. I feel privileged to help them by designing great spaces for their celebrations. • Of course, I realize some cultural institutions must allocate their resources more conservatively than their commercial counterparts so they can channel more support to their core activities. Although any designer will readily agree that you can do more with big budgets, he or she will also admit that making the most of available resources frequently produces highly creative and successful results. • I should add that designing a cultural event calls for the same level of planning, budgeting, scheduling, designing, and project management as any other event. I like to learn as much as possible about my clients and their guests, the nature of their events, the type and sequence of activities in their event programs, and the venues where they and their guests will assemble, if not in their own facilities. Since cultural institutions are intricately intertwined with the larger life of communities, I am always careful to handle cultural events with the same diligence and diplomacy expected by any other client. Why should special occasions dedicated to fighting cancer, promoting folk dance, expanding literacy, and other good causes deserve anything less?

BLACK & WHITE BAROQUE

I was honored to join other fellow New Yorkers not long ago in designing the environment for a fund-raising event sponsored by DIFFA, the Design Industries Foundation Fighting AIDS. Within a large loft at the Skylight Studio, an old industrial space in the Tribeca neighborhood, I created a classic dining room with a modern twist to fill a ten-by-ten-foot booth. I used only black and white elements. If that sounds limiting, take a look at the finished booth. For the backdrop, I backlit grey Lucite® panels that I silk-screened with a black baroque pattern. To set the table, I assembled all-white clusters of orchids, anemone, and gardenia as high and low centerpieces, and contrasted them with all-black vases, candelabra, and acrylic tabletop. I had the silver silk table skirt appliquéd with black velvet in another baroque pattern, Art Deco chairs with black seat cushions, and a dinner service of black, white, and clear pieces. I filled out my concept with a ceiling and floor in black Lucite®, and suspended a custom chandelier in—couldn't you guess?—black and white with clear crystal chains over the table. Perhaps my greatest source of satisfaction, however, was just being able to be alongside such names as Vivienne Tam, David Rockwell, Ralph Lauren, Baccarat, and Skidmore, Owings & Merrill.

A SUPERSTAR BIRTHDAY

Brava, brava, brava! In January 2009, the music world gathered in New York to celebrate the 75th birthday of legendary mezzo-soprano Marilyn Horne and the 15th anniversary of the Marilyn Horne Foundation, which Ms. Horne established to promote the art of the song recital by supporting young artists. Can you imagine how honored I felt to design special settings in two landmark venues for this happy occasion? The event at Carnegie Hall, "Celebrating Marilyn Horne," featured a stellar cast of vocal artists along with rising young singers who have won Marilyn Horne Foundation grants, all performing selections from Ms. Horne's repertoire, ranging from Bellini to Verdi. Because a simple embellishment was all Carnegie Hall needed, I decorated the stage with two large sculptural floral arrangements set in ornate, gold-leaf covered classical urns and pedestals, combining roses in different colors with exotic green cymbidium orchids and forsythia branches.

For the dinner that followed at the Plaza Hotel, attended by friends of Ms. Horne and supporters of the Foundation, a more elaborate response was appropriate. I established a color theme of fuschia and orange by filling the Plaza's ballroom with guest tables covered by fuschia damask overlay tablecloths and gold chairs in fuschia chair covers. On the tables, I assembled low floral centerpieces in jewel tones with purple hydrangeas, Vanda orchids, peonies, roses, raenunculus, and purple lilacs, setting them in crystal bowls and surrounding them with crystal votive glasses to add richness, sparkle, and elegance to the grand ballroom—while evoking diamonds to honor Ms. Horne's 75th birthday. I completed the design by decorating the napkins with fuschia and orange double-satin ribbons and hot pink roses.

MENU

Black Mission Fig Tart
Caramelized Garlic and Leeks
Layered with Chevre and Rosemary
Salad of Mache & Lemon
Basil-Infused Olive Oil & Balsamic Reduction

Braised Short Ribs
Horseradish Jus, Rustic Tomato
Swiss Chard & Celeriac Whipped

GATHERING FOR A GOOD CAUSE

Following the United Nations declaration designating December 14th as worldwide International Diabetes Day, the American Diabetes Association sponsored an event to honor the declaration and heighten public awareness of the global nature of the affliction. In the space I designed for the occasion, I dramatized the idea of nations joining forces to fight diabetes by creating a high-profile image of the earth employing a structure of stretch fabric and Lucite® illuminated by battery-powered LEDs. Of course, the search for better treatments and a cure for diabetes is about people as well as medical science and technology, and I made dramatic use of floral arrangements to highlight their importance. Portal-sized arches of flowers welcomed guests to the event, and there were seven different designs for centerpieces at guest tables, one for each continent, to express the beauty and fragility of the human condition. Needless to say, the overriding message my client wanted to communicate was about optimism, determination, and inspiration in the face of adversity, and I was gratified to see that my design helped achieve that goal.

LIVE THE ~~DREAM~~ Life 2007 GALA

American Diabetes Association
Cure • Care • Commitment

SWINGING INTO THE GOOD LIFE

I recently had the privilege of designing the American Diabetes Association's event, "Swing into the Good Life," a forties-inspired evening featuring swing music and dancing, for the Art Deco interior of the fabled Waldorf-Astoria Hotel in midtown Manhattan. To successfully serve the Association, I had to simultaneously acknowledge the hotel's exuberant Art Deco architectural forms and express the lively yet more restrained Art Moderne spirit of the 1940s. I found color to be the key.

Things became more intriguing in the elongated Grand Ballroom, with its tall windows draped in blue and gold damask curtains and its ornate coffered ceiling decorated with a gold panel design. Here I toned down the ballroom's palette with a silver-gray taffeta overlay tablecloth that perfectly suited the forties theme. Then I grouped large martini glasses with a bouquet of white calla lilies as centerpieces and encircled them with floating candles, not only echoing the Art Deco architecture but also complementing the height and elegance of the ballroom— uniting two different worlds for one "Swing into the Good Life."

A STUDY IN CONTRAST

Simple gestures can communicate a rich vocabulary of meanings, as I was honored to demonstrate in an event designed for the American Cancer Society at New York's Cipriani 42nd Street. In this vast, dignified Beaux Arts former banking hall, I created tall floral arrangements featuring sprays of white tulips as the centerpieces for the tables. While the height of the arrangements commanded a presence in the space, their purity of color and delicacy of form provided a ravishingly beautiful contrast with the monumental neoclassical architecture of stone and terrazzo.

CORPORATE EVENTS

IT WASN'T LONG AGO WHEN DESIGNING AN EVENT FOR THE business community simply involved creating a floral piece for the table. Nothing more was wanted or needed. In fact, even the largest corporations routinely worked with low budgets to achieve modest goals. Business hosts and guests generally found the results quite satisfactory. • In recent years, however, the global economy has intensified competition for customers and market share, obliging corporations to redouble their efforts at winning and retaining business. Corporate events have adopted a more promotional atmosphere as a result. Designing today's corporate event calls for a visual environment that is consistent with the host's brand as well as the milestone being observed. • Since corporate events now play an increasingly important role in business life, their presentation has to be more impressive. Of course, any party must be conducted in good taste, make guests feel happy and appreciated, and express the host's message clearly and memorably, all within a carefully defined budget and timetable. But today's corporate event design—from floral arrangements to the whole active environment, including architecture, interior design, lighting, and sound—should also be seamlessly integrated to form one dazzling and persuasive experience that could only come from the corporate host. • Since branding is key to standing out in the corporate crowd, I like to develop each event environment by combining a company's logo and other signature signs and symbols with a theme that relates to the special occasion. Not only does this set the mood for the day's activities, it gives guests a sense of anticipation. To help my clients visualize and understand my design concepts, I record my creative ideas and vision in drawings and models they can use to work with me in tailoring the event environment to their agenda, budget, and space. • Every project I do is as different and unique as my clients are. It's not a question of budget or scheduling alone. Who are you? Who are your guests? What are you trying to convey about yourself? Where is the event being held? What will happen during the course of the event? The answers are as important as your business and the milestone you want to celebrate.

USHERING IN A NEW ERA IN ATLANTIC CITY

Atlantic City will always remember how the rules of the game changed with the opening of the Borgata Hotel and Casino, bringing high-end, Las Vegas–style design, gaming, and entertainment to the Northeast. I'll certainly never forget the arrival of the Borgata because I was commissioned, along with Chicago's top event planner, Paulette Wolf Events and Entertainment, to create the environment for two weekends of grand-opening celebrations.

Without any suggestions from the hotel for its huge ballroom, I proposed design concepts varying from low to high floral pieces with the goal of introducing a clean, chic, cutting-edge, Armani-style look. The Borgata chose my image of a simple, square, and structured low floral table centerpiece complementing a square table with a natural linen overlay tablecloth. I planted roses in a bed of wheatgrass and highlighted the arrangement with candles and encased pillar candles to give each table a coolly understated centerpiece with a splash of color. To complete the effect, I transformed the standard ballroom chair by attaching a rectangular structure made out of PVC pipes and slip covering it with the same linen fabric as the tablecloth for a square-shouldered look that matched the square table. The whole room came to life as a sea of cool white galaxies whose brightly glowing centers played off white curtains, dark wood wall paneling, round lampshades, and a deep coffered ceiling, proclaiming the birth of Atlantic City's newest star.

Borgata
HOTEL CASINO & SPA

Chopped Crispy Greens with
Yellow and Red Tear Drop Tomato

Orange Tarragon Vinaigrette

♦ ♦ ♦ ♦

Black Angus Filet Mignon, Port
Wine Jus Reduction and Lemon
Nectar Glazed Chilean Sea Bass
with Broken Yukon Potato
Borgata Farms Vegetables

Fresh Sliced Breads and Butter

Cool Lemon Layer Flan
Lemon Cream, Pistachio Cake

A LUXURIOUS HOLIDAY TREAT

How would you recreate the holiday season as celebrated by a prominent New York family during the Gilded Age? I was delighted to give a traditional flourish to a modern design for a leading international bank at the Frick Collection's magnificent Beaux Arts home. Guests were able to catch an early glimpse of the event to come in the entrance hall. I placed a large, beautiful, all-red holiday floral arrangement in an ornate silver urn and set the urn on Italian brocade overlay tablecloth as décor for the guest cards table. Think of this as the bow atop the gift box.

To convey the holiday spirit in the main event space, I used the color red as the connecting visual motif by placing four different sizes of red, hand-blown glass vases on a red lacquer tray at the center of each table. I then filled out each floral table centerpiece with a lush arrangement of deep, rich red flowers, including mini Calla lilies, tulips, mini cymbidium orchids, mini roses, and anemones. You might think this outpouring of nature's gifts to the season needed no further embellishment. However, when I placed everything on a tablecloth of rich red velvet with gold dots and surrounded the tabletop with red chairs, the whole design came together like voices in a choir.

WINTER WONDERLAND

No, it's not business as usual when an organization is granted the opportunity to stage an event at New York's storied Museum of Modern Art. When I was asked to design the environment for a leading bank at MoMA, I realized that competing with the museum's iconic masterpieces of Modernism or its beloved and now greatly expanded home could easily appear unconvincing and excessive. A better strategy, I concluded, would be to celebrate what was already there with a modern event design.

What made the Museum of Modern Art accessible to me was its cool, refined, neutral beauty. Handling it as an exquisite blank page, I gave it a personal interpretation of modernism based on white 1950s-inspired glass holiday ornaments I used as flower vases. To complement the artwork on display, I chose blue and white hues to bring a winter feeling to the table centerpieces. Lighted Lucite® tabletops finished the illusion by transmitting a clean look and snowy effect to the entire space.

A FIRST-CLASS AFFAIR

Jet-setters knew air travel would no longer be just another hop across "The Pond" when Sir Richard Branson announced Virgin Atlantic's new Boeing 747 service with first-class seating. Could the event to launch the big jets be out of this world as well? Taking my cue from the venue, Chicago's Illuminating Company, I designed an environment to complement the Virgin Atlantic brand and coincide with the industrial-looking facility.

A clean, cutting-edge tableau positioned at the entrance seemed the right way to greet guests, so I created a rectangular high bar of three Lucite® pedestals supporting a Lucite® top and filled them with organic forms and lighting. The pedestals were decorated with sculptural floral pieces combining earthy and organic materials, and the top displayed flats of wheatgrass with red flowers around the edges. This distinctive object lifted the design and the event itself to a different dimension.

I also included a custom-designed image of cloud-strewn skies and Virgin Atlantic's logo on curving wall panels to serve as an enhanced background for the band and performers, complementing the look for the event with two huge structural floral arrangements planting natural wisteria vines, blue and red colored roses, and hydrangeas to reprise the company's colors. You could almost feel the event becoming airborne even before the band began to play.

ROMAN HOLIDAY

Design Fusion was honored by an invitation from an international bank to produce an event in Rome. Exciting as the assignment was, the logistics of putting on a show overseas represented a challenge quite unlike those of domestic productions. Flower and material supplies, manpower, shipping, and customs clearance were just some of the many issues I had to contend with to achieve success. However, the outcome was extraordinary.

At the Doria Phamphilij Museum, I complemented the classic décor with a modern twist. Upon ascending the staircase, guests were greeted with large vibrant green anthurium, tall white calla lilies, green hydrangeas, and green cymbidium orchids, placed in front of an antique marble statue and muted stone walls, to contrast living white flora against timeless white art and architecture. Think of it as Act One of a three-act drama.

For Act Two, guests saw two bold, architectural arrangements of deep red peonies, vibernum, and cascading green cymbidium orchids in contemporary black trumpet glass vases, my modern twist to this classic setting. The arrangements were fresh and unexpected, yet stylish and respectful. Their presence set the stage for the antique brocade velvet wallpaper and displayed furniture to come.

Guests entering the reception hall of the museum, a high-ceiling space decorated with priceless Italian master paintings, took their seats at tables where the room provided a magnificent backdrop for modern crystal glass candelabras I selected as the focal points for the floral creations. I kept the groupings of burgundy peonies, orchids, and vibernum around the candelabras deliberately low to make sure guests would not have any obstruction. Heavy brocade damask overlay tablecloths were used to match the room's walls, while napkins were simply folded and tied to tiny roses with ribbons, placed underneath plates, and suspended to introduce a modern touch—and a happy ending for Act Three.

Young and old alike, we have all fantasized about exploring a museum after closing hours. The dream came true for a leading bank's holiday party in New York's legendary Metropolitan Museum of Art.

When I saw the grand stairway of the museum, I was inspired to use the beautiful steps to form the company's umbrella logo to greet guests and to brand the entire evening's festivities. It was a big challenge to install hundreds of red votive candles in just half an hour to form the shape. To solve the problem, I made a pattern from clear acrylic sheets to map the umbrella shape step by step. Since then, this solution has become a precedent for work by Design Fusion.

For the main event in the Temple of Dendur, I paid homage to the Egyptian architecture, with lofty floral decorations and dramatic lighting that responded to the Temple's monumental size yet brought the seating area down to human scale. It was important that the materials I used (including papyrus, lotus pods, magnolia branches, and pine needles) complement the Temple rather than obscure it. For the finishing touch, I placed an array of lighted pillar candles in cylindrical glass vases around the perimeter of the pool that flanks the Temple, introducing a reflection on the water and giving an extra glow and timeless serenity to the room.

A CHANGE OF SEASONS

You're probably aware of that famous declaration by the great modern architect Mies van der Rohe that "less is more." While I seldom find this applies to my work, the inauguration of the Steiner Studio in New York's Brooklyn Navy Yard gave me an ideal opportunity to test it.

I was asked to be a part of the design team for this special event hosted by Abigail Kirsch. With the waning of autumn and the arrival of winter, I wanted to impart a distinct, seasonal feel to each of Steiner Studio's two floors. Guests coming at different times of the day would experience the congenial warmth and poignancy of autumn on one floor and the cool, austere elegance of winter on the other. To evoke the seasons, I used such basic materials as birch poles, white hydrangeas, dried and crystallized tree branches, and young maples, combining them with a lighting scheme that washed blue light on columns and ceilings. The one extravagance was the square bar I designed using a profuse arrangement of branches to form a "tree." The client was delighted at the way my design displayed the potential of the space as guests slipped in and out of the seasons just by circulating between the floors.

BRINGING THE OUTSIDE IN

Any Broadway actor, musician, or stagehand will tell you Central Park is nearly a mile north of Times Square, the center of Manhattan's famous theater district. However, a corporate client gave me the opportunity to bring Central Park to the Millennium Hotel Broadway and its historic Hudson Theatre, in the heart of Times Square, for one magical evening. I set the stage for the client's dinner by turning the theater's ticket hall into a park entrance with park benches, lampposts, and trees. Having planted this densely landscaped passage, I abruptly altered the mood by treating the much larger theater lobby, the site of the main dining area, as a clearing in the woods. I chose an arbor-style gazebo with branches of wisteria vines swirling up to the ceiling, trees placed around the perimeter, and dramatic uplighting to evoke the park's canopy. I dramatized the symbolic clearing with illuminated Lucite® tables and Louis XIV–style "ghost chairs." To remind guests that they were dining al fresco, I created a centerpiece using wheatgrass as a runner, surrounded by sunflowers and floating candles, to span the entire length of the main dining table. Just imagine—the Great Lawn just steps from the Great White Way.

DECK THE HALLS

Even jaded New Yorkers are impressed by Renzo Piano's airy and sunlit modern addition to their city's legendary Morgan Library and Museum. When I was invited to design a corporate holiday party in 2007 at the reinvigorated Beaux Arts landmark, I decided to dramatize the new world of transparency and light to tie the event to the architecture. Beginning with groupings of Lucite® tables and chairs, I added tall glass candlesticks and sparkling glass bowls for the flowers. Of course, you can't build an entire event on "nothing," so I splashed bold strokes of red flowers into the picture, evoking the company's logo, a warm touch that drew smiles from guests.

CELEBRATING IN THE MOONLIGHT

The cool white of new-fallen snow, fresh milk, and a full moon inspired me to transform the ballroom of New York's Marriott Marquis into a chic, soothing, and clubby space for the New York Marriott Annual Awards program. I grouped tables with illuminated, milky white Lucite® tops on aluminum frames to form squares and triangles that made the room glow, ran a floor-to-ceiling white drape to encircle the perimeter of the room, and suspended hanging square lamps of sheer white fabric to define a

second, lower ceiling. The details I chose reinforced this scheme, including ice acrylic chairs and frosted glass chargers that complemented a table setting with a simple yet elegant white floral décor, white orchid garlands draped from the lampshades, and understated lighting that let the radiant tables define the space.

Innovative, unique, geometric and highly architectural in treatment, these two illuminated clusters of tables form a square and a triangle, introducing guests to the new trend in table setting. The tables cast an ethereal spell on their surroundings. I emphasized this point with contemporary floral pieces featuring all-white cymbidium, calla lilies, and hydrangeas in pewter vessels placed on square trays. Is this how we will all be dining out in the not-too-distant future?

GOLDEN HARVEST

In the foyer of the Frick Collection, on New York's Upper East Side, guests of an executive party, held at the height of the Northeast's fall colors, were greeted with a lush arrangement of cascading flowers that emphasized the warmth of the golden harvest season.

To stage the scenery of autumn's colorful foliage, I treated the event environment as an extension of the artistic masterpieces surrounding it. Guests were welcomed with floral tributes to the season, starting with two boxwood topiaries decorated with orange mini-roses and hydrangeas at the entrance. The glow of autumn subsequently led guests into the main dining area, where lush, low centerpieces in rich yellow, gold, burgundy, apricot, and amber hues, decorated with finely detailed faux wax pillar candles, provided a climax to the seasonal salute, enhanced with embroidered deep brown silk taffeta tablecloths that matched the fruitwood charivari chairs. Finally, chocolate napkins decorated with chili peppers from Mexico—representing the nation honored by this event— yellow cymbidium, and apricot roses accented the copper chargers and wrote a lovely coda to the festive imagery.

INSPIRATIONS

FLOWERS ARE BEAUTIFUL, DELICATE, AND SHORT-LIVED — yet far more powerful than most people realize. I know this from experience, because I've learned first-hand what flowers can do for the most colossal of public spaces as well as the most intimate of private chambers. When combined with other plant materials, as well as anything else we might imagine, they can alter their surroundings as easily as they can complement them. Whether they're incorporated within a total environmental design or featured as self-contained art at the centers of guest tables, floral arrangements can be remarkably expressive. • In the following pages, I invite you to share my joy in using flowers as a medium of artistic expression. The forms that my arrangements assume directly reflect the needs of my clients and their venues. At times, traditional bouquets of flowers in vases are all that an event requires. Then again, contemporary, three-dimensional structures of flowers and other materials are increasingly taking their places in more adventurous events. • My clients are always welcome to talk as much or as little as they like about the floral arrangements I design for them. Even if they can't name the species of flowers that interest them, I can usually understand what they describe to me and identify one or more particular flowers that correspond to their hopes and dreams.

ACKNOWLEDGMENTS

My deepest appreciation goes to the following people who made this book possible:

Bob Perlstein, Esq., and his wife, Marianita, for making my dream come true.

Moon Lee for capturing the most stunning photographs imaginable.

Roger Yee for putting my vision into words.

Leslie Stoker and Kristen Latta of Stewart, Tabori & Chang for their patience and editorial work.

Susi Oberhelman for turning this book into a work of art.

Joel Facultad for his work and dedication to my company.

Anthony Dennis Josue for always being there to give me a helping hand.

Preston Bailey for introducing me to the world of event and floral designs.

Paulette Wolf Events and Entertainment, Inc., for trusting my talent

Bonnie Walker Events for believing in me.

Melanie Arden Cirulnick for collaborating on some projects with me.

Bill Ash, Joseph Cozza, Michael Lotwich, and Dr. Victor Vicente for their kind support.

Philip Ong for his graphic art contribution.

Erico Chan for sharing some astonishing photos

Roméo Enriquez for the helpful advice.

Efren and Berta Dordas for extending their generous assistance in Rome.

Marilyn Horne for appreciating my artwork and lending her words.

My most sincere thanks goes to all my dear friends, individual and corporate clients, vendors, and suppliers who have contributed to the success of my business career. Without their whole-hearted support, I would not have had the opportunity to utilize my talent and create.

CREDITS

All photography by Moon Lee except the following:

Pages 22–25: Photographs by Eric Chan

Pages 43–45: Photographs by Philip Ong

Page 234: Photograph by Sarah Merians Photography

Page 6-7: Project in collaboration with Melanie Arden of Melarosa